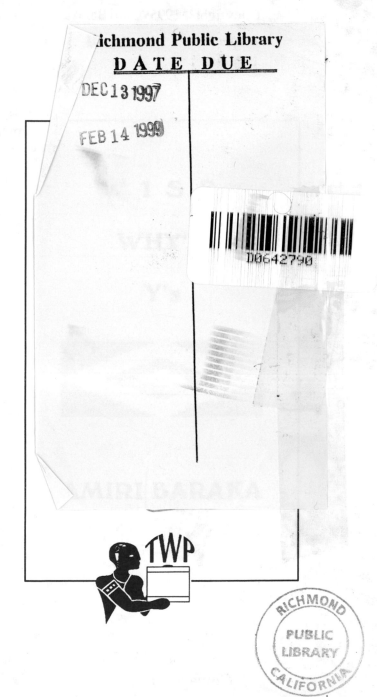

ISBN: 0-88378-150-6 (cloth)
0-88378-047-X (paper)

First Edition
First Printing 1995

Manufactured in the United States of America

Cover art by Tom Feelings
Cover design by Angelo Williams

Third World Press
P.O. Box 19730
Chicago, IL 60619

Introduction

Why's/Wise is a long poem in the tradition of the Djalí (Griots) but this is about African American (American) History. It is also like Tolson's <u>Liberia</u>, WCW's <u>Paterson</u>, Hughes' <u>Ask Yr Mama</u>, Olson's <u>Maximus</u> in that it tries to tell the history/life like an ongoing-offcoming Tale.

Wise, Why's, Y's

W I S E
WHY'S
Y's

Djeli Ya
(THE GRIOT'S SONG)
(1-40)

Each of these sections is accompanied by a piece of music. The work is meant to be visualized by painters Vincent Smith and Tom Feelings.

Before *Wise1* there is a long improvisation, not yet completely transcribed. It is called, in its entirety, *PRE-HERE/ISTIC* Sequence: It is divided like this—

DAT—*Africa*   (Drums-RWalker)

DEUCE—*Ghost (Snake Eyes)*   ("*Space Spy*"—
                                     Moncur)

TREY—*My Brother the King*   (3/4 solos & Dun
                                     Dun)

FO'—*Railroad of African Bones*   (Under water
  (Box Cars)   African Funeral
                                     Music)

FI'—*I Aint From Here*   (*Wade In The Water* Afro-Xtian Lament)

WHY's Intro: NOBODY KNOWS THE TROUBLE I SEEN Traditional (Trombone Solo)

Wise 1

WHY's
(Nobody Knows The
Trouble   I   Seen)
Trad.

If you ever find
yourself, some where
lost and surrounded
by enemies
who won't let you
speak in your own language
who destroy your statues
& instruments, who ban
your oom boom ba boom
then you are in trouble
deep trouble
they ban your
oom boom ba boom
you in deep deep
trouble

humph!

probably take you several hundred years
to get
out!

Wise 2

(Billie's Bounce)
Charlie Parker

I was of people
caught in deep trouble
like I scribe you
some deep trouble, where
enemies had took us
surrounded us/ in they
country
then banned our
ommboom ba boom

the confusion
the sickness

/What vision in the blackness
of queens
of kings
/What vision in the blackness
that head
& heart
of yours

that sweet verse
you made, I still hear
that song, son
of the son's son's son's
son
I still hear that
song,
that cry

cries
screams
life exploded

our world exploding us
transformed to niggers

What vision
in the blackness
your own hand sold you
"I am not a king or queen," your own hand
if you bee of the royal catch
or the tribes soulwarped by the ghoulishness

I still hear those songs and cries
of the sons and sons and daughters and daughters
I still bear that weeping in my heart
that bleeding in my memory

And I am not a king
nor trader in flesh
I was
of the sufferers
I am among those
to be avenged!

Wise 3

(Hipnosis)
Grachan Moncur III

Son singin
fount some
words/ Son
singin
in that other
language
talkin bout "bay
bee, why you
leave me
here," talkin bout
"up unner de sun
cotton in my hand." Son
singing, think he bad
cause he
can speak
they language, talkin bout
"dark was the night
the ocean deep
white eyes cut through me
made me weep."

Son singin
fount some words. Think
he bad. Speak
they
language.

'sawright
I say

'sawright
wit me
look like
yeh, we gon be here
a taste.

Wise 4

(Dewey's Circle)
David Murray

No coat has I got
no extra chop
no soft bed or favor
no connection with the slaver

dark was the night
our eyes had not met
I fastened my life to me
and tried to find my way

talk did I hear
of fires and burning
and death to the gods

on the dirt where I slept
such talk
warmed me

such talk
lit my way

I has never got nothing but hard times and punishment
Any joy I had I made myself, and the dark woman
who took my hand and led me to myself

I has never got nothing

but a head full of blood
my scar, my missing teeth.

I has never got nothing but
killer frustration/ yes dark
was the night
cold was the ground

I has never got nothing, and talk
of rebellion
warmed me

Song to me, was the darkness
in which I could stand
my profile melted into the black air
red from the flame of the burning big house

in those crazy dreams I called myself
Coltrane
bathed in a black and red fire
in those crazy moments I called myself
Thelonius
& this was in the 19th century!

Wise 5

(Breaks)
Baby Dodds

I overheard the other night
standing by the window
of the big house

a nigra say, through an alabaster
mask, "the first negro
was a white man."

Slanty red darts angulate the darkness
my hands got cold, my head was sweaty

like a mystery
story
like a gospel
hymn
like the tales
of the
wizards
and the life
of the gods

I did not know
who my father
was

I only barely
knew
my mother

14

But I knew something that night
about a negro
something even
the tv cant wash
away

I fount out something
about the negro

the wind may blow
the train dont come
the mayor might belch
his mistress might gain weight

But I fount out something that night
about the negro
& the world
got clear

you can hurray all you want to
you can kiss an elephant's ass

But I fount something
that night, before I slid
back to the field hands' quarters
I fount out something
about
the magic
of slavery

& I vowed not to be
a slave
no more.

Wise 6

(Jimmy's Blues)
Grachan Moncur III

Has we come far?

We has come far.

How we got there

How we got where?

Who we talkin bout?

What they name?

Oh, the slave peepas
you the slave peepas

Who the slave peepas
Just the same.

Struggle in dark, come down
the road. Knew your life
your sorrow. Knew your singing
in the dark. Knew the whip

that scarred you. And the century
change, alright, alright, the
years go by in light in darkness

there's white peepa voice behind my air
claim I should be free. They peepas hang out
in the north somewhere, dont need no bread
from the big house man. They voice hang
in the air.

But thas alright, alright wit me.
I preciate all of that.

Thas alright, alright wit me
But I been gone, naw, I been gone

my shape look like black on black
and fading.

Wise 7

(The Four Man)
"Papa" Jo Jones

Back in the forest

the maroons laid

outraged by slavery, & split

from it, when the bombs burst

across the air, and fire tore

mens hearts, they knew some new

joint change was upon the time

and so emerged, a gun in one hand,

something funky, in the other.

Wise 8

(Mojo Hand)
Lightnin' Hopkins

From the country
to the City, we left
where things
were pretty—to get away from
the klansmen, and race freaks who
hung with the Slavemasters' cause
who could not believe in democracy
who could not let life be beautiful
who howled moon shadows screaming
for the primitive. Who climbed the trees
for past centuries, hollering for caves
and blood. From the country, to the city
we left where things were
pretty. Got city life, got city bred
wanted rights and services (get to that,
we thought) when all the time
it coulda been better, when all the time
new cdda been, built cdda been, progress
cdda been, and all the great notes of peace
all the great notes of peace
     all that
        cdda
          been.

Wise 9

(God Don't Never Change)
Rev. Pearly Brown

our war
was for
liberation
to end
slave times

now war
is over
we free
they say

who they
who say
what free
gone be?

there are cities
we can go to

there are cities
of light and newing

So what these faces laws hover
these swine wind law death people
these death time rebs return to crow
these slavemaster corpse leap off the flo
these sheet face coward monster haints
these death word carriers and slave lovers

there was war
before
be war
again
died before
will die again
but not gone die
not gone leave
not gone cry too long
not gone grieve

free is who we are and be
love who what will lift us we
struggle love struggle—against primitive death
while you walking round
spirit death tie you down
slave death and servant death and let me work for us to be.

Wise 10

(Do, Lord, Remember Me)
Rev. R. Wilkins

So in 1877 the lie grew
we all knew
the heart dead
the lie instead

They talked blood
They put on hoods
They paid for murder
They closed the books

No democracy
No light
primitive times
return

Across the road
the horse men prowled
American guns for African American lives

You'll never vote
you'll never grow
you'll never never never never
be free   never
be free
          never
be free

Amiri Baraka

never

　　　never
　　　never

　　　　　Enter Booker T.

　　Poison, Jordans,

The Kneeled Supplication.
　　A last blackmail.
　　A calling of hypocrites.

By daylight a seared
　　forest, church of the night
　　give way to lash rhythm

　Cotton executions.
　Live stock butchered,
　Henry Bibb gone again-

　　Our books our lives
our north star humming
on the other side

Waiting for the fast thing
Day starved, night blistered
at light speed

　　Cruising the collective mind
　　No footsteps, it uses
　　Fire for its everywhere.

Rough Hand Dreamers   (Wise 11)

(Milneburg Joys)
Jelly Roll Morton

"I, myself, happen to be the Creator (of Jazz) in the year of
1902."
                              -JRM (Ferdinand Le Menthe)

You was a country folk, on the
land. Farmers before farmers
founders of cities, Ile Ife
where the world began. Was creator
of university, I trumpet timbuctoo
because I cannot bear to think
you think Banneker was wilder
than the breed. It was the women
conceived of familiar cows and
architecture. Yon drummers know
how they are hide curers & musicians.

Now they enter the cities to enter future
reality. Now death, now blood, now hooded
criminals, resistance in its human dimension
like electric theories, post all abrahams.

What was it we wanted = Ourselves!
And why? We had been inside others being alive
for nothing

and worked to death
our murders
were circuses
our murderers
something like
clowns.

Why's 12

(High Society)
"Old" George Lewis

A farmer come to the city

dirt growing in his mind
songs black land come into
curl your poetry blind
Banjo
waves and sinking bones
play eyes on sky
blood music

heaven people
say see heaven
they seeing
up side down

now they say we fought for evil
took our guns, the wise ones hid, say you
never was to be here
you never was to be

kept to edge of city
alleys behind the bossman's
house. got a job, you got a space,
you got a bond to heal your face

changed from slave
to convict, gone

from lazy to vagrant
jail lost boy in sleep
jail house/plantation moan
jail, was how they changed it

we
   vote among roaches.

Why's 13

(Mr. Pinetop's Boogie)
PineTop Smith

And now you know
how "ghettoes"
grow

(you knew
how ghettoes
grew?)

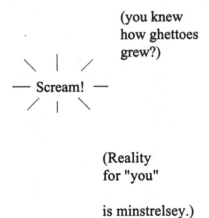

— Scream! —

(Reality
for "you"

is minstrelsey.)

The Stranger   (14)

(Didn't He Ramble?)
B. Bolden

Here he come
dirty bum
bloody sun
on the run

our lives, yes, "God"
our lives

there is nothing
only suffering

all the rain
is only
pain

our lives, yes yes
our lives
City came
turned insane

on the streets
whipped and beat

our lives, yes "Lord"
our lives

-2-

What was
was cool

What was
it?

Good times
soon, yes, soon

Laws re came
eyes and brain
was the same
turned us lame
Where was what
we wanted
at?
In how
In who
& why?

Turned black
& white, Kill Africa
again. Liars
& preachers &

horrible
creatures

Thats why I say "F---
          D.W. Griffith!"

An apt slogan for
the dreamers
when the dreamings
done

(notes)

    1877 Hayes-Tilden
    1883 Civil Rights Unconstitutional
    1896 Booker T. Washington
    1897 Separate But Evil
    1915 All lies and no wise

the daring roach vote
is dead in the streets
The "White Primary"
had replaced the good ship
"Jesus"
except
there were
always exceptions
                except

So now we know
ghettoistically
speaking
the passage
from 19 to 20.

The lines were drawn
from exclusion
to separation

Kept us
at our station

American Express!

    You! Slave-
a blind light burn

      you! you!

aint no slave

but aint no

citizen
neever

    You!
(a sound rings like)
echo
in the
woods

You! No word
  to replace
  what is correct
  w/what
  is torture fruit

You!
      vagrant
      ward!
      half animal-
      sub species
You!
      Booker T.
(Jesus pray for me)

You! no word
   to describe us

   black nigger
   will do

        *

I hum
I sing
I used to know
every
thing

I cry
I lie
I came from out
the sky

So be
& see
another
family

You free
dont say it
you free
dont play it
you free

But perhaps we shd not stutter
our temper in the wind
like this.
        After all
        (a long pause
        for the sky writers'
                clause)

There are the steps of
years in tune with—
of strengths inside
the "boys & girls"

these steps like clouds

tree
tops
voice-
sez

The speakers, the good niggers
the growing mind of we
self
there really was and is
an Africa

an African
an African in
Americas

There is no slavery
but that which
destroys us

Tho it be a chain
on our arm
or brain

*

I cant go to them conferences
no more
& see wilting petty bourgeois
salespersons

arty christ arty
sure
& Lana Turner too.

Eating tidbits
of foolishness
healthy fools
sicker n
sicker

I knew niggers joined the Muslims
after Malcolm
died
who sd they'd dig
him up

& bury him
again

I knew niggers
holy as washboards
fat & bald & betitled
rapist
torturer
greasy junky

"Is it true"
                     (an interview)
that machine gun
in yr front room
is for other

spooks?

Yawns inside the
jailhouse
walls

Walks the campus
proud

I'm tired, I say
of being there

w/ the fleshless
the hairless
the mindless
the heartless

saying the same
wrong
song!

*

So we didnt
tell you the whole
story

Battle Royals
Assassinations
Assignations
Furor

How WEB
took on
Booker
T.

How the 20th c
finally
came

*

    & when it did
this lurking madness
Democracy
was
all
but
dead

    xcept
(& there are always
    xceptions)

    Inside
     our
    head!

It's just that
what had happened
Senor
was more complex
than
Semple.

(But thats
another
story)

Just hear by the rush
hours into
centuries
the mad family

waits, in constant
motion,
there is such a thing

as
Africa

Its in the real
world

& its
got

seeds.

What about Literature? W-15

(Creole Love Call)
Duke Ellington
(Sidney Bechet
Version)

Fred D., my
main man
had tolt all
up there
How he scaped
& got to out
side, straight up
slavery
days

My man
Fred, was
trying
to move
us
too

"Go on,
         Go on"

This trans/lation

    speaking
    in
    tongues
         p66-67 SNarratives
& there were others
both sisters
  & brothers

      List
      Names

             Equiano
             Roper
             Brent
             Brown
             Pennington
             The Crafts
             Bibb
             Rahahman
             Montejo
             etc.[1000]

    "You are loosed from your moorings, and are
free; I am fast in my chains, and am a slave! You
move merrily before the gentle gale, and I sadly
before the bloody whip! You are freedom's swift-
winged angels that fly round the world; I am
confined in bands of iron! O that I were free! O,
that I were on one of your gallant decks, and under
your protecting wing! Alas! betwixt me and you,

41

the turbid waters roll. Go on, go on. O that I could also go! Could I but swim! If I could fly! Is there any God? Why am I a slave? I will run away. I will not stand it. Get caught, or get clear. I'll try it. I had as well die with ague as the fever. I have only one life to lose. I had as well be killed running as die standing. Only think of it; one hundred miles straight north, and I am free! Try it? Yes! God helping me, I will. It cannot be that I shall live and die a slave. I will take to the water. This very bay shall yet bear me into freedom. The steamboats steered in a north-east course from North Point. I will do the same; and when I get to the head of the bay, I will run my canoe adrift, and walk straight through Delaware into Pennslyvania. When I get there, I shall not be required to have a pass; I can travel without being disturbed. Let but the first opportunity offer, and, come what will, I am off. Meanwhile, I will try to bear up under the yoke. I am not the only slave in the world. Why should I fret? I can bear as much as any of them. Besides, I am but a boy, and all boys are bound to some one. It may be that my misery in slavery will only increase my happiniess when I get free. There is a better day coming."

> Till the explosion came
> they sang toward

We never go back
> (for long)
> Only
> forward

This is the stage of
    our Du Bois

& his the bulwark
    of us
    our saying & thinking
        articulator
            of our
            insides

            true
            measurer
    of these
            outsides

            link from Fred
            & he now dead

And under the sun
my boy
there is the thread
of track
where we runners
spin
fast faster
than
light

Can you see
the baton? (Well
    Feel
     It!)

From Fred to E.B.
    to Langston
    to (Zora to Richard & Ted &
          Jimmy &)
              Margaret
  to
  WE!

A NOTE TO
PRESIDENT PASADOEKEEOH!
& His Wise Ass Reply (16)

(Ramblin')
Ornette Coleman

For this
for nothing
it dont swing
it cant sing
    ahrgh!
      hell w/ numbers
        & Barons
        & sun spanked lip
          of
          corn

    Oh Say
    we can

MURDER them
    can you
    See
      Oh
    Say
    we can
    you
      See
      MURDER

porter
reekin'

VAYA CON DIOS
contraption

constructed of
pomade sculpture
shoulder pads
horsies
whore sees

                        (A RAY GUN)

Ho Ho!
Hum
  Ho
    Hum

  (it was america
that patch
unner
the desert

  the parchment
red
upside
down
sd
"Nigger"

(He Replies)

stop dancin
in the wind
feet aint touchin
the ground

I've beat
   you
   &
   hung
   you
   &
   sent yr
   picture
   round

Stop dancin
Stop wigglin

I am Elvis Nightingale
Jim Crow Señor
president Wilkie's ghost
Lincoln's bullet hole

Rachel Sumner, a "wide girl"
Mason & Dixon
August Cream
Don Lee

& Maulana bug out

Pressure Dude of these
   Uncreated
      Vacancies!

   & I spit

               power
          yr toes light up
      to salute spookarabian
        bandito

   So quiet
    its silence

   murders best in the
     no sound
      dark

No we aint givin up La Isla
    Encantada
      nor
  E.116th St. either

the shorties are coming
the interesting crazy people
murderers name
         Boutique Buddy
         Expensive Earl
         Stiff Siff
         Underwater Turncoat

Left Friend Ball-No
Up under stairs shivering-Johnny
Joey with the dumb wife
        & other
        flags of our
Holy light

    I want to splain
      you in
      yr lank witch
      Ham
      & Cheese
that I is everybody's
    Daddy
Every booties
    Pirate

& the No for every
    Yes!

Now are there
      questions?
                (transmission
                   weakening)
You, in the back
    row

OPEN FIRE!

Individualism As A Tourist (Y's 17)

(Eccentricity)
James P. Johnson
Newark, N.J.,
1918

He's showing me
his theories. Theories
of the
Night
Bat & vampire
theories
Blacula
theories.

A sunrise beholds us
passing through
our lives
completely dumb?
Full of surprise
In chains
as modern as
    airplanes

Descendant of old eyes
you think it was easy
to jump the animal track?
        Cultural nationalism
     is what "the antelopes
     play," in their discouraging
herds.

And I dont want
his theories
old landscapes

I cd get drunk
    on the air
    I dont care
    My skin is brown
    My mind crisscrossed
    in time, a history
    book
    Plus, I am a
    Musician.

Where the slave wanders
he knows he's free
yet not being free
defines
him

he wants a family
& he has one
he's got babies waking
in the
woods

When he escaped
they sounded an alarm
inside his feeling
a chime inside
his
mind

That's why he was staggering
an excess
prophet
he was no lone

Ishmael no vanished
Ahab
Slain in nature
scowling &
one eyed
but a legislator

conga player
2nd baseman
field slave made bad
blinking
in the morning

early there
smelling the new day
before the others
& way off from them

     singing
     blues laws

     beginning to operate
     the sun among the leaves
     its breeze the news
     of wars to come
     & plenty of work.

REPRISE (Not)

(Nutty)
Thelonius Monk

Not you
Not him

Not us
Not we
the lone slave sings

how cd he know
slavery is over
that its the 1890's
& while he's been flying

the Slave Narratives, blk
& white abolitionists
Fred Douglass, Walker's *Appeal*
Nat & dem

(White John
was Brown!)

Hostilities, actual cannons
& deaths, politics
as usual
how cd he know

on a hill in the sun
morning duets
Henry Fonda had set
him free
in the next flick

that 186,000 of him
bled or were murdered
by poor dumb hunkies
battling for their own weakness

How cd he know
in his post light speed
funerals everywhere
Niggers trailing the army

Appomatox
Emancipation
Jefferson Davis
In a Sour Apple
Tree

The lone slave
singing while flying
above the green spotted
land.

The power
& Glory
The 40 acres
An old story the revolution
gone bad

Its powerful enemies
restored by more
powerful
enemies

How cd this distant laughing figure   *(Jackieing)*
the trees & red sky passing   *T. Monk*

realize
it was
the apple he approached

(He was never
reconstructed
he was high
naturally)

The Klan he took
as maniac prehistoric
reptiles, & butchered them

The Union troops receding
toward the picket lines
& victrolas
He was hip to Edison
The portable he carried

was small
w/a tiny aerial
these poets & painters
beautiful women he loved
a best of times he wanted

Darting toward a jumble
of color
& syncopation
he was thinking
about Duke

letting that organization
of sound
lift him
& lower him

How cd that lone slave know
someone thought
he was cheap labor?
there *was* work
to do

Only when this dark
period was over
1876-1915, yet to be
battered, attacked & bled
left again, Africa

for dead
what he cd see
looking down from
that blue sky
was swinging

It lived in New York City
there was a train
got you there.
He was thinking
about

organization.
We needed, he hummed,
some kind
of
Renaissance!

Y's 18
(Explain' The Blues)

Ma Rainey
("Georgia Tom" Dorsey)

What are
these
words

to
tell
it

all?
          facts
          acts
          Do they have
          their own
          words?

          !Exacts!

   The Scientist in love
          w/precision
     but we need
      this
     we must have
      it
     the exact real
     the concrete

what it is
   && that whole
   is story

Africa
Slave
mind memory
Birth
A land across
     the ocean
Blue Water
Green world
     Blood
& Stopped Motion

These mixmatched slaves
they cooled
readjusted
the black
     forever
the white
     till the debt's
     paid
     (for them to
        become
        as new
        as we
        so they
        become
        the overseers)

this world of
    limits
    twists
    & opposing
      forces

these elements
of constant
Change

What is yr world
& yr face
yr clock's
  confession

Have you slept w/
    the constitution
    3/5ths of the darkness
    spoke to

refer to the records
thereby
dumb romance
it's lie
for a flag's
    health
a class
stealth
    to cover
    its murder
    its beatings

As a domestic
   bleeding

   a near by
   tragedy.

We cd go to Dred Scott
   for testimony
   Henry Bibb

We cd ask Linda B
   or Henry
   The Box

We cd be drawn into
   eternity
   w/David and his
     Appeal

To speak of all
   we have
   feel!

Only reality
   say
Where we will
   go
It's tethers
It's chains
It's sick pricks
   inventing
   crushings
   for our lives

a decoration
of horror
they cd define
& understand
they cd justify
our deaths
& torture
they cd be clean
& taking
a little

taste

As the lightning
tried to illuminate
Animal life

Their smiles even
chill us
mad poseur
posing as
the mad doctor
who is the original

American
Nazi
The southern Himmlers
& Goebbels, baked
in our dying

What the war
    proposed
        our entrance
        as citizens
        who once had been
        slaves

This 13, 14 & 15 yr numbers
        in the
        lottery

This Freedman's Bureau
this 40 acres

        as grounds for
        identical
        social
        valence
        political
        economic

            (not Sociology & Social Democratic
                political
                Bohemianism)

Revolution, The question
        the answer

What revolution
  cd not be
    destroyed
    bought
  or postponed?

What revolution
  cd not be
    sold out?

All those
  in the real
    world

all those
  that have
    actually
    been

The betrayal of Niggers was necessary
  to welcome
    Imperialism!

  That was its condition
    The Killing of
      Nigger
        Democracy
So Spain
  it's decorated
    past
The Philippines, Puerto Rico
    Cuba, the booty

The new era

    amidst our sunlight
      mass laughter
      emancipation
       The Paris
        Commune

The Berlin meeting to divide
    the Dark Places
    Colonial Pie

What the Slave Trade
      Wrought.

   That one day the Heathens
wd actually come on the real
side—that they wd take our
hearts as funny valentines

That they wd stick our lives & history

in the toilet bowl
     (toxic
     waste)

& claim our
   past
& future

As the Commune
   smashed
   dead

The rehearsals
   for Buchenwald
   & Belsen
carried out in the
   American
   South

Unwilling nigger actors
      Heavy
      Minstrels
      this torture Birth
      of the

      Black Nation

The "rule by naked terror"

can not be called
   Fascism

because we
   are
Niggers

& that
is too
famous
for the likes
of us

Fascism
   wd come later
   in Europe
   (naturally)
   & be well advertised

   as an excuse
   for Israeli
   imperialism.

#19
Death Parallels

*(Work Song
Take This Hammer) Trad.*

Understand
the life
Spiral. Infinity
Stood up on its
head
(tail)

it all
comes
back
on "higher
ground."

These conflicts
(for instance)

are centuries
old!!

Sd it was gone
but
here it come
again

until
the scrawl of Western
Man, a dude
name Fred

who had peeped
the whole basket
of scorpion future
Slave to K4

Dont under cover
our sh--
The details get lost
The substance the big boys'   *(Work)*
hide   *Monk*
but you dont
you want to get the
real deal down

Dont fade
Spade, or wait
for divine
nothing
to speak

lace chains
sun baked
& final

we felt real & moving
forgetting, making notes
healthy anyway, for looking
& hoping to be so much
even from slaves and renegades
our warm color one day
to tell?

The African
      The Slave
            The African
                  American
that journey
profound as a Mo
fo - mind transportation

I want to tell
      it
      I want
            it down

I want its feeling
centuries of
what was burning
in the slave
mind

eye blast
music under

funk halo
work & that
is slavery
work & that
is/ murder

it's not a
    history
       chronicle

        dit dat
        date
        detail
        the Grass
        the specific
        twist

(Tho thats
to come
the Science
the concrete
Analysis
of concrete --

But how to *go*
& carry
our Whole life
    what does it mean
    to f---
    w/history?

I want little ones to comprehend
& the mature, w/o reference
or theory, stone reality

understood-

> How is it rolled
> down
> > What
> do you
> > carry?
> To speak
> of it
> all?
> What do you conjure
> how deep in its crazy
> pit?
> > To dig up,
> What tells it all
> > The precise
> > sunset
> > &
> > rise
> The look
> in an old man's
> > eyes

I can lay out a field
  a Spectrum
     Where in

So what is spoken
  is the living
     the flesh
      & its
           Movement—

Slavery
Civil War
Reconstruction
its
Destruction
   The Slaves'
   poverty.

20
Borders (Incest) Obsession

(Steal Away)
"Sorrow song" Trad.

The Slave is obsessed
  w/ being Out!
  Air charms
    hum
    a song.

If I were this slave
& had run thru centuries
      for centuries
  in search of my Free
     Self
  Borders wd not
  obsess me

  freedom
  wd!

There is that love story
  I told ya bout
  that shadow angle
  pool player

elegant thumbs
are the light
  that describe
    us

Gradually we become history
    to
    have

    us

    inside
    it

There was 19th c Progress
    Slavery ReBorn

as fascism
in its colored low budget
original
version!

We are bullets into
    tomorrow
  We are Changerers

these limpid blues
that packed sky
(the lost keys of
    which
   like my own
   dry frenzy

is the part of the hatred
  that's good
    for us.

   O Slaves dare we
Stand & Murder Slavery

at the point its foot
upon our back
is the final *terrific*
detonator

From beneath the
    brawling shadows
of the monster's legs

Map fiend Wood
   shadows
blood shadows

dialogue dead people
   their cynical
     quiet
    the burn

in the constitution
for who is it that
will not worship celebrities?

    Now they send us
      a declassed
    Movie Ham
    Himself Adored!!

          An Inferior Star!!

    As the box cars line up

       a jig to their hang

    the insignia changed
    But murders still the game

And who is more famous
      than Hitler?

Now that the next
      roaming Empire

    is about to subside

    Exploding Exploiters!

"The People must be
      Christianized!"

In time for
      the latest crusade
  & Inquisition

White
    Christian
        America

A torch in hims
    hand
No brain - heart
    connection

the newest dead direction
Ghost Murderer

& the greasy lighting

    of Death!

    Oh Ghost
    Who Has To Be
      A MURDERER!

      Vulgar
      Steel
      Children Chewer

"Crime Has Paid,"
    you scream

Yr Belly speaking
  Caribbean
  Spanish
  - - -

The Slave Master
Always Attacks!

  Always!

They wanted 3/4 ers
  of the Union

   the slave empire
 Stretch down
   to Northern Mexico
 Suckup Cuba
 Slave Colony Nicaragua

The Duck

in a Conk
Philadelphia, Mississippi

The Same language

The Empire Cycle
Go
Down
They dont
Admit it
But it so
The Empire Cycle
Go
Down
& Down
to GO

But it
Got to
Got to
Go

Railroaded by Time
We were always
trying
to remember
things.

Life,
an epithet!

*

Therefore,
>Be Guided
>By MOTION!

>(Honest Human)

We are travelers &
>travailers
>Here!

Let the verb
of what it is
inform your
hipness

GARVEY
Y's 21

(C Jam Blues)
Duke Ellington
(Performed w/
Louis Armstrong)

We wants to
   join
      somethin

w/ Relishes
on they head-heart

Red wearing
Green needing
Black being

Somethin.
This is 1919,
we live in
        Harlem

Blues fell by

is here
amongst us

& southern
speech

flows out
   Penn Station

     Funk
took the

    rails -

We wants
   to join
     somethin

Somethin
     make us
        Stronger
Can get up
   off the
     ground

Somethin Red
   with a Green
   sparkle

And Black!

History-Wise #22

(Black Mountain Blues)
Bessie Smith

"The only
       railroad
              guaranteed
not to break down!"

100 years
       Before
       The Col-
          trane
              The
       real
       sub
       way
                     Ms "Moses'" Streamliner
                     John Parker's Darker
Sparker
at Night
No light
but a far star
North

& way off
Like a whistle or a horn

The black night
fills
our ears

We gon' go
has already

gone

"Choo Choo" is the translation
in somebody else's

Station

#

Whoooooooeeee Whoooooooeeee
Whoooooooooeoooo Whoooooooooeeoooo Whoooooeeeoooo

is its real
sound

from way up under
the ground

Way
Down

Whoooooweeeee   Whoooeeeoooooeeooo
Whoooooeeeoooooeeeooo

Thats it real
sound

84

Under Ground!

& then sometimes
if the night is cold
& bright

that whistle cries
like all through

that night

that whistle cries
& it moans

Whyyyyyyyyyyyyyyyyyyyyyyyyyyyyyyyyyyyyyyyyyyy'sssssssssss
    Whyyyyyyyyyyyyyyyyyyyyyyyyyyyyyyyyyyyyysssssssssssss
        Whyyyyyyyyyyyyyyyyyyyyyyyyyyyyyyyyyyyyyyy
            &c.

The Y #23

(Potato Head Blues)
Louis Armstrong

House
like
this
    Prairie skies
    Indian Bones

darkness visited
now here forever

    Promise skies
    Sunset silence

grey is light
now
void
is light
now
    History bleeding history bleeding
    1929, death on time

    Garvey gone.

Conversation In A World (24)

(Black Horse Blues)
Blind Lemon Jefferson

That way
the blues comes

like a sentinel
of the world

Why the blues
comes

The blues
Wise
Music

Full
of
Why's

And hundreds of millions of
cries

—GO OUT THEN!

Blues
can leave inside

& Blues
can sit on a bench

outside
on a cold blue

American
Day.

Blues Loves Magic
Itself

The dark crazy character
with the funky

Sinister
laughter.

My
Man

Blue life rhythm
stalking

our days
& our nights.

(25)

(<u>Hambone- Trad.</u>)
Archie Shepp Version

<u>WORD   PAINTING</u>

<u>WORDPAINTING</u>

1929: Y you ask? (26)

(Chime Blues)
Fletcher Henderson
piano solo

In "The Masque of the Red Death"
near the end
of the ball
a deadly stranger appears.
Not Vincent Price,
Some thing with eyes like numbers
mouth a siren about to wail
Screamed headlines, the dope of the radio.
The party goers freeze
the Butlers and Maids get their notices
they are skeleton walkers, boat feet,
Wings, dark countenanced baritones
Willowy sopranos; the hall
Swept with an actual tide
of Red & Black—The White
is the silence as the Flag Waves.

Did some one say, "The Renaissance
is over?" Or was that the living
Dying wind, reality, or the Rags
of yr future? The living dying wind
adhesive against wet w/ blood top hats
souls w/bullet holes. Ex leapers smashed
against the bankruptcy of bullszit & oppression.

Finally we know, half superiorly,
all these guests
will die of the Plague. The Black Death!
The Red Death! The Plague!

Horror movie statistical murders.
Dead in old houses

& under cars. In chain gang Gulags
& share cropper concentration camps.

Most of us wake up in a crumbling
plague ridden mansion.
Imitation music
Imitation laughter
Imitation people
w/ Imitation Lives-
A nation of minstrels
and ignorant powerful people
plus slave niggers almost as insane
as their
oppressors!

A ritual of Black & Red Caped
Devil Messengers
In the shadow of the casement glass

Our glasses, raised in the air,
are frozen
in a shadow
as wet
as blood!

It begins to snow outside
beyond the dead forest,
inside the naked empty grey cities

The snow is spotted w/ blood.
A madman's signature
is shown on television.

Disease, now, is
continuous!

19th Century Moment -- Y's Up   (27)

(...Pallet On The Flo')
Mama and Jimmy Yancey

Fire
in the dark

A Crown
or
Eye
Move faster toward it

Life /

War
&
Death /

Freedom

We want Life,
   Freedom!
      War & Death
      We leave
for their
lovers.

We push on
Sisters
&
Brothers

Fire
in the Dark

Fire, Fire
In the Dark!

Un Y's (28)

(Christopher Columbus)
Fats Waller

Not only
    Slavery:
Beast History

    SLASH!
Preach loyalty to Concentration Camps!
Our Grandfathers saw them as Ghosts & Cannibals
        prepared for the KKK
    They wd turn Philly into Hiroshima
      to keep Niggers in they place.
    Beast cannons, from the left and right.
Between slavery & fascism
      only a deep breath.
        what passed
            for Reconstruction

Stellar Nilotic (29)

(You Gotta Have Freedom)
Pharoah Sanders

You want to know
how I escaped? (There were bright yellow lights now, and red
flashes.)

Can we talk here? Are we all ex-slaves? (a laughter
ruins the dawn silence, and the birds acknowledge us
with their rap of flutes.)

That star, just over the grey green peak (the moonlight
acknowledges us and makes us shadows.) Was how I was led,

A slender black woman, around 23, put out her hand, turning
toward the star. You know how night is, the star was blue and
beautiful. Around it music, we drummed through the forests.

Their ignorance, that country of "Their" and its united snakes,
unified in madness, and worship of advantage. You cannot
have aristocracy, except you have slaves.

They teach you that.

Yet our going, our breathing, the substance
of our lives, was with us chanting
against whatever was not cool.

This was always, and remains
a foreign land. And we are

undoubtedly, the slaves.

There is some music, that shd come on now.
With space for human drama, there shd be some memory
that leaves you smiling. That is, night and the way/
Her lovely hand, extended. The Star, the star, all night
We loved it
like ourselves.

You Wants To Know Y? (30)

(Caravan)
Juan Tizol/Duke

What you must
  deeg
can it be sd
you
can
is that
BeBop is
scat
is
African
American Bloods
Speaking still
pure African
Shoo bee doo bee
Wheeee
Africans
& Flyin
(Cross oceans!)
Home.

At The Colonial Y They Are Aesthetically & Culturally Deprived (Y's Later) (31)

(Maple Leaf Rag)
Scott Joplin

SHARK MONSTER Rockefeller
        Codes. Explosion is War.
        For Wha? (The Blood)
                Profits
                    of New
Avant disease   come to ya'
What was in the bush / yr society
        smoked
        EATS EATS
            its terror
                    White Beast
            alive w/ Harpoons
inside it the bones
of whole nations

Slavery, Concentration
Camps, Plantations
Gas Chambers

The death of Reconstruction was
    the death of the dream
    the death of the reality
    The death of any wd be American
        Democracy!

Bloodless "Jaws" whale shark monster
it kills include cultures
now post McCarthy where
is Grapes of Wrath or I Was

A Fugitive or the truth
of itself? Was Sam Spade
a Communist Sympa
thizer? Or Philip Marlowe?
But even that individual cry
for straight shot Democracy
cd finally find itself banned in darkness
while Robotic Horror pornography makes us
consumers of masturbation and degenerating
   values.
              An america where the only academy awards
              go to Ronald Reagan w/ Clarence Pendleton as
              Ben Vereen. "Boogity Boogity" an
              Ellison description of Ellison describing.
              The teeth of imperialism is a chant
              for the dying things needing to die.
              Its poison swelling EAT EAT
              Its cry of terror!

You see (a whispered
        aside)
     even its "humanity"
     (a people of slave holders)
     was a kind
     of minstrelsy

An unconvincing
Black Face Act.

Now the flicks are a form of Commerce
   less and less
     of art
  Film innovation was revolutionary
Eisenstein's Red Montage
  With that connection, the tech
nology & casual populist dream

  Equality.
  So much popcorn.
The Jews, Italians, Irish, Poles, & c.
  had first to give up
  being that
to enlarge the baby slave holder
  Fat banker fish
to be its evolved "revolutionary"
  Sleek sea thing
    (Sleek?
  A nigger
  in its teeth
The feed of bulging monsters
so creative they invented
fascism in the black belt
of democracy
So the Black Face, Dixie Land, thin rag, non-"race,"
    Funny hat, Paul Whiteman
    stiff seat, noun baked non swing
    of the "cool," bebop's cover.
    Or for the Shorties & Rodgers

& Bru's & Becks & the green
of our dollar - oh man- to
the "progressive jazz" of glass
adjectives w/ no where to blow.
Until we get fusion & its con
a cool out of new blues
      turns a chain to a flexible
      rubber unbreakable straw
      for yr elevator colored nouveau,

      to the gallows garden
      of the floating compradors

      where their eggs, like body snatcher
      pods lay hatching way in the middle
      of the air.

      This bend of class
      to the death of itself
      & rebirth in fake neon flames.
Elvis Presley was the FDR of
      the 1950's, the philosophy
      was workable & when the
      Beatles moved in simply slander
      them w/belittling Jesus
      & enlarge the American market.
      Nigger Music became figure
      music. Chocolate death
      Plastic. Instead of rejection-
The Huge monster's mouth
Him/Her's protein digesting skin

To Europe? To The Past?
But leave reality to the
real & the living

By the end of the 19th century
they cd convert the sorrow songs
to Barber Shop
Quartets.

W WHY-EE-EEE! (32)

(Strange Fruit)
Billie Holiday

We cd hear
the licks
& hear Mrs.
  Hamer
          Screaming

They got two black inmates
to beat
her
as well

("No one responsible for those attacks
was ever apprehended") Ch. 13

"Do we have a Justice Department?"
She wailed,
          "or an injustice
           dept?"
But the church
do teach ya
how to sing

"We have been black powerless people
for four hundred years"

"I've seen black people
boxed in"

"& the rats
eatin on the people"

"This country was built
on the sweat
& blood
of black people   (—F.L.Hamer)

Sd Cochise,
"They will spill yr blood
like rain!"

"There Was Something
I Wanted To Tell You. " (33)
Why?

(African Lullaby)
Babenzele Pygmies, S. Africa

Revolutionary War
 gamed
       sold
            out
                 The Tories
still in control
of the culture

English Departments
still
& the money & "culture"
in an "English"
accent.

The Green Mtn Boys
Tom Paine The Bill
of Rights

tried to cut
it

But then 19th centruy
Explosion, Free the
Slaves, Kill feudal
ism, Give rights
to the Farmer & Worker

the vote to Women

But that got blew
     Hayes-Tilden, Bloody
          Democrats

     Traitor
     Republicans

The Ku Klux Klan
(A murder Gang!)

& that leap, into industrial society
democracy they sd
Got all but Killed
     tho murdered
     many times!

Marx, Engels, Lenin, Stalin, Mao, Ho
     Fidel, Nkrumah
     Martin, Sandino
     & Malcolm X

Have all been
betrayed

All revolutions bear their own
betrayal, & betrayers

The world is complex
its reality materially
simple

It is the dying of the life

the quenching of the spark
the greying of the light
the cold whiteness of the recently
full of flaming inspired intelligent
heart! The dead entrail of our
       collective traditional
       enemy. Animal
       connections. Metaphysics.
       Greed. Anti Science
       lives. Ugly in power
       and uglying up our only
       life.

The rot, the lie, the opposite
will always, if there is ever
that, exist. As life means death
and hot cold. Darkness lights'
closest companion. Its twisted,
       & rises as a spiral. It is No &
Yes, and not It for long.

Motion, the beat, tender mind
you humans even made music.
But, our memory anywhere
as humans and beyond, parallel
to everything, is rise is new is
Changed, a glowing peaceful
Musical
World.

What betrays revolution is the need
for revolution. It can not stop in life.
Whoever seeks to freeze the moment is

instantly, & for that instant, *mad!*

We are servants of life in upward
progressive motion. Fanners
of the flame. Resistance is Electric.
Fred sd, its measurable on every
block.

The wd be stoppers of revolution
are its fossil fuel

Winter comes
and Spring

We can sometimes
hear
explosions!

WAR (A Y-er) #34

(*Down By The Riverside*)
Mississippi Shieks

Some nights voices
wd slip out
the old testament

The book wd glow
neon blood red
in the dark.

Like drums speaking
light flash meants.
Voices in sorrow unison

Canvas too soaked in death to
    drift in silence
    in the wind

Chained tones, invisible blood clones
    bleeding dawn & twilight
    a wire through ears & eyes

Death had no disguise
    Resistance pulse
    Poison, Jordans,

The Kneeled Supplication.
    A last blackmail.

The Kneeled Supplication.
    A last blackmail.
    A calling of hypocrites.

    By daylight a seared
forest, church of the night
give way to lash rhythm

    Cotton executions.
    Live stock butchered,
    Henry Bibb gone again-

    Our books our lives
our north star humming
on the other side

Waiting for the fast thing
Day starved, night blistered
at light speed

    Cruising the collective mind
    No footsteps, it uses
    Fire for its everywhere.

YMCA #35

(After The Rain)
Trane

We talked all the time
    as spirits we were
    allowed.
      & watched the different
      primates in their turns
      & elegant twists

We caught the rising virus
    like a style of neon
    murders. A calm
    blood washing upward

Between giggles & drunk laughter
    wisdom hit the walls
    & ceiling, windows
      closed if open
      opened if
      closed

It was never quiet
    no familiarities
    were permitted

The good guys sat
    & watched the door
      the wizards crawled
        from 14th St to the
        outer crust

Colors & rain
The well dressed well spoken
The poverty stricken
The lonely
The important
maniacs

They were singing through their
noses, & fingers
Everybody was a headline
A massacre that cd not
be a revelated gorilla

These were rich people & Heroes
The stink was not stink, the garbage
not really garbage. If you cd bend concrete
& hang like the high tent of drunken rapists
Applause wd rock & roll you in yr dreams

Awards could be coughs
hands reaching
poetry of climaxes
proposed. Crippled

Weasels I knew
& sang a song
for the airplane
underground

Not to be subjective
a heart full of dashes
no opening through backs
exploding in their
dreams.

It is not enough to witness, you are
   somewhere anyway
      & you wont sweat.

2

Riding through the valley
   Sundays coldness a hole
      in summer. A red dark ball
      pasted over
        with notes

But picture The Tempts
   Do-walking
      clean among black
      waves

Picture a blinding whiteness
   like Cab Calloway's
      shoes

the nigger computers
   bluely reporting
      ghosts ahead
  who are cannibals

We ponder for the Bop-trillionith
   time

      The Madness
      of the Gods

Amiri Baraka

The Turn Around Y36

(The Turn Around)
Hank Mobley

Jack Johnson

        was convicted
  of White Slavery!
  He was probably
the only person ever
convicted in this
      country
        of Slavery!

-Coyt's Son

("One More Time")

(Humph)
T. Sphere Monk

Likewise
in all these years
I only seen one time
Downbeat called somebody
a "racist" from the front cover
& that was LeRoi Jones. Was
the only time.

-Likewise

115

Lord Haw Haw
(as Pygmy) #37

(All Blues)
Miles

We were here

> *before*

> God

> We

> *invented*

Him.

> Why?

That's a good/ god damn
question.

Why Don't You Fight?
#37 (One Mo' Time)

(Black and Tan Fantasy)
Duke Ellington

I am
the Missing
Link.

This sad society
     pornography rocket

       Yr deaths now
       sure to be
        comic

No longer led by even
     the abstractly
       wise

Not even
     a champion
     vampire

The joog factor
     ice pick
     in yr bleeding
       brain

(Black, Brown and Beige)
Duke Ellington

You've heard the poets, felt
    Jacob Lawrence
    & Riviera

Understand the sheer
angle of rushing pleasure
    smile
    learn

The spin inside Puente's pop
    Blue horizon
    in Trane

Animals should not
    be running
    our lives

I want a human chance

    Your house
    Stinks

dead things
w/ bloody bones
collect around yr
thinking

The Poor
The Smashed
Slaves
Ignorant Gods
    Static
    ideas
    like money.
Brand us all as Jungle Bunnies

Blinking at the sun
tormented by volcanoes
& earthquakes

depressed
w/ colds &
Arthritis. Wiped out
    by incredible idiocy
    starvation
    drought
    greedy primates

No, it's a stupid world
    You've made
    an ugly
    one

If I did not fall
    in love
    w/ beauty

I'd be cooler
   (the / year?
   the state?
   the lie?
   the newspaper

 As an aesthetic exclamation point
Think of music
    as the only
          soul
          God
          cd
          have

Singing slaves the
      slaves
Singing

They sing   Africa   spiritual
              scat   blues
                     rag
                         swing

    they want
    tomorrow

    lost
    yesterday

  pain today

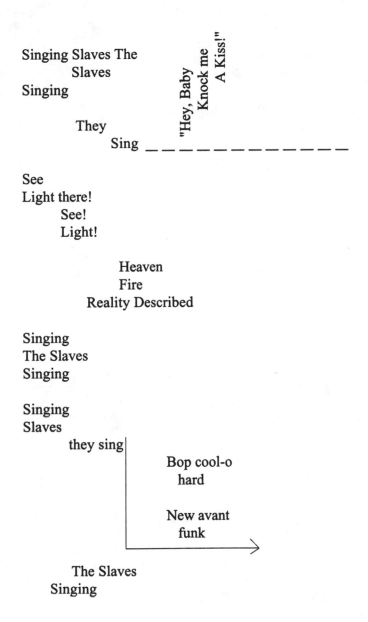

Singing Slaves The
      Slaves
Singing

      They

         Sing

"Hey, Baby
Knock me
A Kiss!"

See
Light there!
    See!
    Light!

        Heaven
        Fire
    Reality Described

Singing
The Slaves
Singing

Singing
Slaves
    they sing

        Bop cool-o
        hard

        New avant
        funk

    The Slaves
  Singing

Religious history air
    & pain & struggle
      there
        The Slaves, Singing
          Singing

          Singing

Speech
#38 (or Y We say it this way)

(Be Bop)
Diz

OoBlahDee
Ooolyacoo
Bloomdido
OoBopShabam
Perdido Klackto-
    Veestedene
Salt Peanuts oroonie
    McVouty
      rebop

Ornithology
BaBa Ree Bopp

Ooo Shoobie
    Doobie

& The Sisters
Dooie Blah
&
Dooie Blee

a Kuka mop

Bee Doop Doop
    ie Doo
      pie   -Lemon Drop
    Be Doopie
      Doop Dop

Squirrel
in The Glass
    Enclosure

of the essential
Transbluesency

We dreamt Paradise
    w/ you
    Naima

Savoying
Balue Bolivared

in black Night
Indigo

Brownie Red
Hollywood Hi Noon
        Trane Lights

    Salaam Thunder
        electricity trademark

Yr heart
in Repetition

            de Milos

Monk's Shades

made the tru/man
of a Hairy
   Square
   symbol
in faded corniness

Gold Electric
Natural Grace
   like
      Freedom

 Horns
of our
 Description - Desperatenesses'
       Drums

Sharp spectrum Blace
    painted hard light

Lush life romance
   ancient
     trade.

Hideehideehidee hee
ooooohhhhhhhhhh

  Oh Imperial Ghost
  who is no
   Ghost
  & Real

Autumn
I think of you

& the sorrow
of gates

& absences in your soul
   America
   like the dead

   spaces

  like ignorance

between the

   stars

        -

The Ape said,
"Floogie,
  Lucy, Baby!"

Human light
 in your
  African
    Eyes.

Travelin Travailing
Majestic
Life Form

Scatting

Boogieing

Cosmos In

Cosmos

Rhythm

Rapping, capping
hand
slapping

Black Poet

Chanting

to the 1st fire.

So The King Sold The Farmer #39

(Angels & Demons At Play)
Sun Ra

The   Ghost

    Ghost

Watch out

    for the Ghost

    Ghost get you

    Ghost

    Watch out
        for the
    Ghost

In bitter darkness screams sharpness as smells
  & Seas black voice
Wails
in the death filled
darkness

Their bodies disease beneath intoxicated floors
A seas shudder afraid its turned
            to Blood

The bodies
    they will, in death's skull
    to Lionel Hampton
Ghost   Look out
        for the Ghost

Ghost
    is have us
    chains
    is be with
      dying

      is caught

Sea mad, maniac
        drunken
    Killing sea

                    Ghooooooooost

                    Ghooooooooost

The chains
    & dark
    dark &
      dark,   if there was "light"
             it meant
                Ghooost

Rotting family we
    ghost ate
        three

A people flattened chained
    bathed & degraded
       in their own hysterical waste

below
beneath
under neath
deep down
up under

          grave cave pit
          lower & deeper
          weeping miles below
              skyscraper gutters

Blue blood hole into which blueness
is the terror, massacre, torture
    & original western
        holocaust

      Slavery

     We were slaves

      Slaves

      Slaves

Slaves

–

Slaves

–

Slaves

—
   We were

Slaves

—
Slaves

—

  They threw
  our lives
  a way

Beneath the violent philosophy
  of primitive
   cannibals

  Primitive
  Violent
  Steam driven
  Cannibals

R R

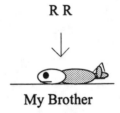

My Brother

Y The Link Will Not Always Be "Missing"
#40

(The Wise One)
Trane

Think of Slavery
    as
Educational!